SANTA FE'S HISTORIC McKENZIE NEIGHBORHOOD

A Contemporary Look at Old Architecture

PRAISE FOR *Santa Fe's Historic McKenzie Neighborhood*

"This book should exist for all Santa Fe neighborhoods. It is a visually stunning guidebook for those who love to discover the hidden architectural treasures of Santa Fe and those wishing to stay and dwell here."
—Pat French, co-founder New Mexico Historic Women Marker Initiative and French & French Fine Properties

"As a Santa Fe native, I appreciate how the creative imagery in this contemporary look at historic architecture confirms that Santa Fe is and has always been a lure for the most artful, creative and passionate people; and for that vital reason, we must love and protect the architecture of our marvelous city. Victoria and Cal's collaborative work captures the fundamental nature of Santa Fe as I know and remember it in my childhood memory. This particular neighborhood is home of my all-time favorite Santa Fe building."
—Lisa Samuel, ASID, IIDA, NMLID #313, owner Samuel Design Group

"This wonderful book values the McKenzie House, where I practice law, and a full spectrum of structural design spanning more than a century in this mixed residential and commercial area. Thanks to the combined efforts of government, the Historic Santa Fe Foundation, and people like the artists who authored this book, the historic fabric of this unique neighborhood is being preserved for future generations."
—Robert and Ling Hilgendorf, owners McKenzie House, Historic Santa Fe Foundation Registry

SANTA FE'S HISTORIC McKENZIE NEIGHBORHOOD

A Contemporary Look at Old Architecture

Victoria Rogers and Cal Haines

Introduction by Stuart A. Ashman,
former Cabinet Secretary of Cultural Affairs, State of New Mexico

Historical Text Contributions by David A. Rasch,
Historic Preservation Division, City of Santa Fe

SUNSTONE PRESS
SANTA FE

© 2011 by Victoria Rogers and Cal Haines.
All Rights Reserved.

No part of this book may be reproduced in any form or by any electronic or mechanical means including information storage and retrieval systems without permission in writing from the publisher, except by a reviewer who may quote brief passages in a review.

Sunstone books may be purchased for educational, business, or sales promotional use. For information please write: Special Markets Department, Sunstone Press, P.O. Box 2321, Santa Fe, New Mexico 87504-2321.

Library of Congress Cataloging-in-Publication Data

Rogers, Victoria, 1951-
  Santa Fe's historic McKenzie neighborhood : a contemporary look at old architecture / by Victoria Rogers and Cal Haines ; introduction by Stuart A. Ashman ; historical text contributions by David A. Rasch.
    p. cm.
  ISBN 978-0-86534-813-4 (softcover : alk. paper)
 1. Architecture, Domestic--New Mexico--Santa Fe. 2. McKenzie Neighborhood (Santa Fe, N.M.)--Buildings, structures, etc. 3. Santa Fe (N.M.)--Buildings, structures, etc. I. Haines, Cal, 1950- II. Title.
 NA7238.S364R64 2011
 720.9789'56--dc22
                              2011013831

WWW.SUNSTONEPRESS.COM
SUNSTONE PRESS / POST OFFICE BOX 2321 / SANTA FE, NM 87504-2321 / USA
(505) 988-4418 / ORDERS ONLY (800) 243-5644 / FAX (505) 988-1025

The artists at work in the neighborhood.

Contents

Introduction—9

Preface—13

Visions of the McKenzie Neighborhood—15

Street Names—39

Map—41

Historical Perspective—43

Architectural Notes—45

Acknowledgments—51

About the Artists—55

INTRODUCTION

Stroll through the historic McKenzie Neighborhood of Santa Fe, New Mexico and feelings of nostalgia and reminiscences of a past era are conjured up. However, the compacted diversity of brick and adobe buildings, pitched and flat roofs, and elegant porches on cottage and territorial style homes in this three-by-two-block downtown area are not typical of the Santa Fe streetscape. For many whose focus is the culture and preservation of our town, the images in this book offer an intriguing perspective.

The collaborative work of Victoria Rogers and Cal Haines advances a long tradition of artists inspired by New Mexico's special character. As residents of this historic neighborhood, they approached the architectural mixture with a daring poetic filter. While numerous local and regional organizations work to restore and preserve Santa Fe's historic structures and museums celebrate photographers and painters of the Native American and Spanish-influenced styles, this collection aims at re-visioning history through using nontraditional line and color to present a contemporary look.

This is a lesser-known neighborhood in the heart of Santa Fe, settled by community movers-and-shakers during a time when the goal of style was to look and be yet another piece of Americana. Fortunately, the rest of the city undertook an architectural style that now distinguishes the McKenzie Neighborhood as unique and precious in its way of evoking small town America and bygone times.

    A simple walk in any season creates a contemplative mood for those who decide to wander there, just a few blocks from the bustling Plaza. Once you look through the images and fascinating documentary details in this splendid publication, you will be compelled to discover, as did the artists, new possibilities in what you see.

—Stuart Ashman, former Secretary of the Department of Cultural Affairs for the State of New Mexico, Director of the New Mexico Museum of Art and the Museum of Colonial Art in Santa Fe, New Mexico

Artists' Staab Street residence and studio.

Preface

Living in a historic neighborhood of Santa Fe, New Mexico means seeing how the past weathers time, some of it gently fading and some deliberately preserved. Our personal lives are laced with ongoing curiosity about the area's earlier settlers who, through the centuries, designed and constructed homes, worked, raised families and aged here. On a practical level, residency leads to learning the city's rules and regulations for any new building and remodeling that contributes to keeping the character of a rich and varied heritage. Once this was wide-open New Mexico territory, and as is typical near the center of a town's commerce, growth gradually filled it in. The withstanding architecture represents the progressive generations of available materials, options for comfort and popular style.

  The artwork, which is the core of this book, developed as unpredictably and collaboratively as the miniature settlement surrounding our 1920s Craftsman Bungalow. What began as an inner-vision of one especially charming nearby house evolved unexpectedly into a yearlong exploration on paper of the unique personality of one after another of the old buildings. Their spirits surfaced beautifully through contemporary mediums, freed by the fresh and surprising outcome inherent in the collaborative process. On closer examination by David A. Rasch from Santa Fe's Historic Preservation Division, research revealed that aside from a purely artistic appeal, each image in our collection depicts different details noteworthy for their historical context.

    We realized that binding our prints together with background material would speak to lovers of art, Santa Fe, historic architecture, guidebooks and books as art. The pictorial aspects of our work matched with real, documented lineage allow the mind to wander contemplatively between the mysterious and the known, the past and the present. While we may live—or visitors walk—amidst all that has preceded us, it is with today's eyes that we appreciate and transform, revere and renew our experience of someplace with as many possibilities as our immediate world.

    Here's a word of explanation for the reader. This book was designed with an aesthetic emphasis, presenting the images with minimal text distractions and arranging them in order of date created. At the same time, the book is meant to invite casual touring of the McKenzie Neighborhood in Santa Fe, to enjoy identifying and learning more about the buildings and area that inspired the artwork. As we chose to respect the owners' privacy, the designation of each building is given by its district and lot as shown in the New Mexico Historic Building Inventory Form. All of the McKenzie Neighborhood is in SFHD #1 (Santa Fe Historic District #1). With no street addresses to go by, the viewer must seek a bit to find. Inside your book is information to enhance the journey of discovery. There is a section about the history of the street names, illustrated with a spunky map. The Architectural Details section cross-references with the images' SFHD and lot number, and points out each building's structural and style elements in a meaningful historic context.

—Victoria Rogers and Cal Haines

Visions of the McKenzie Neighborhood

Victoria Rogers and Cal Haines

SFHD #1 Lot 14
Built pre-1882.

SFHD #1 Lot 20
Built circa 1902–1908.
Addition 1930–1942.

SFHD #1 Lot 15 and 16
Lot 15 built 1927–1929.
Lot 16 built circa 1930–1942.

SFHD #1 Lot 23
Built 1902.
Addition 1948.

SFHD #1 Lot 73
Built circa 1913–1921.

SFHD #1 Lot 71
A portion built by 1890.
Remodeling and additions begun 1934.

SFHD #1 Lot 72
Built by 1890.

SFHD #1 Lot 82
Built circa 1941–1943.

SFHD #1 Lot 18
Built circa 1902–1908.

SFHD #1 Lot 31
Built circa 1930–1942.

SFHD #1 Lot 58
Front portion built pre-1885.
Back portion built circa 1921–1930.

Street Names of the Historic McKenzie Neighborhood

The streets of the McKenzie Neighborhood were all renamed in the late 1800s or early 1900s for the notable men who settled the area and one admired man of power of the time, Thomas Jefferson. Missouri-born attorney Thomas Catron became an early New Mexico United States senator. William W. Griffin was a federal land surveyor and served on the first Board of Directors of the First National Bank of Santa Fe. James Johnson was a prominent merchant during the prosperous days of the Santa Fe Trail. German financier Abraham Staab—titled "Merchant Prince" by his colleagues—was instrumental in the construction of the St. Francis Cathedral and built a now-famous Victorian house that is part of La Posada Hotel. William A. McKenzie from Illinois—along with Alexander Irvine—established himself in the hardware business and resided in the only living quarters on what became McKenzie Street. Frenchman Placid Louis Chapelle was the third Archbishop of Santa Fe from 1894–1897.

The history of the McKenzie Neighborhood, and the architecture in it, differs from the more widespread Native American and Spanish cultures in the foreground of New Mexico's past. Surely, if the buildings in this area could speak, they would tell many colorful stories about the gentlemen after whom the streets are named.

Several were involved in efforts for completion of the Santa Fe railroad line into the city, laying the groundwork for the new public rail system Santa Fe businesses and citizens have been enjoying since 2008.

Map of the Historic McKenzie Neighborhood.

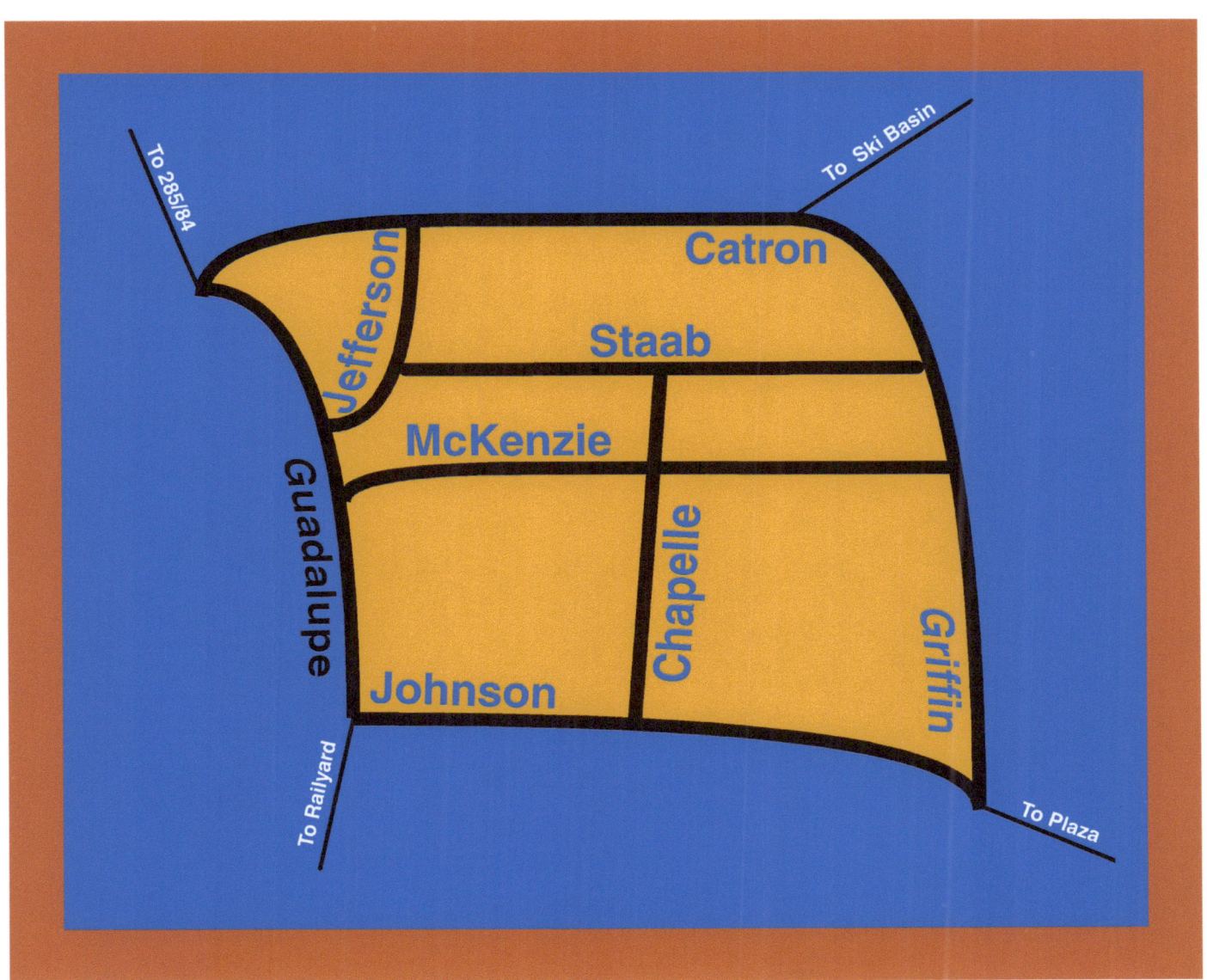

HISTORICAL PERSPECTIVE

Santa Fe's Historic Districts are preserved in a fragile balance between the rural romantic past and an urban sustainably-oriented present. The historic properties stand as monuments to the prevailing tastes that directed architectural styles through various eras of change with their own unique charm.

The western portion of the Downtown and Eastside Historic District, known as the McKenzie Neighborhood, embodies the pressures placed on Santa Fe to look more American during the Statehood Period. Located near the railway depot, enabled wealthy citizens could readily take advantage of new methods of construction for their homes using fired brick, milled lumber, pressed metal sheathing, and larger glass windows. Here, imported architectural styles were harmoniously combined with more traditional adobe building techniques to create a neighborhood with integrity.

—David A. Rasch, Historic Preservation Division, City of Santa Fe

Architectural Notes

In these notes, David A. Rasch describes the historically significant architectural particulars of the real buildings represented in this book's artwork. The full size images are in the front of the book.

**SFHD #1 Lot 14
Built pre-1882.**

The McKenzie House was constructed in the late 19th century with a blend of eastern Victorian Style details on an adobe structure. It was saved from demolition by court decision one hundred years later as an excellent example of Santa Fe's Vernacular architecture.

SFHD #1 Lot 20
Built circa 1902–1908.
Addition 1930–1942.

This early 20th century brick house with a Bungalow Style pitched roof porch was "Puebloized" with a stucco finish and a river rock wall enclosing the yard when Santa Fe Style was popularized in the 1930s and 1940s.

SFHD #1 Lot 15 and 16
Lot 15 built 1927–1929.
Lot 16 built circa 1930–1942.

Here a 1930s Spanish-Pueblo Revival Style building was enhanced with Mediterranean Style details, including a pressed metal tile finish on a gabled roof and a few arched openings.

**SFHD #1 Lot 23
Built 1902.
Addition 1948.**

This rare example of the Decorative Brick Style was constructed by 1902. The rustic brick structure is offset by a delicate wooden porch with chamfered posts and jigsaw brackets.

**SFHD #1 Lot 73
Built circa 1913–1921.**

This wooden-framed Bungalow Style building was given a veneer of brick. The historic 4-over-4 wooden windows have brick window sills.

SFHD #1 Lot 71
A portion built by 1890.
Remodeling and additions begun 1934.

The Escudero House was originally constructed with adobe in the early 19th century. Numerous alterations by subsequent owners through the 1940s include concrete block and wooden frame additions with blended Territorial Style, California Mission Revival Style and Renaissance Revival Style elements.

SFHD #1 Lot 72
Built by 1890.

This adobe home was constructed in the Territorial Style with brick coping on the parapets and milled lumber shutters. A quaint white picket fence encloses the lovely gardens.

SFHD #1 Lot 82
Built circa 1941–1943.

This early 1940s Vernacular building is a humble example of the simplified stepped massing that characteristically gives a human scale to the Pueblo Style.

SFHD #1 Lot 18
Built circa 1902–1908.

The California Mission Revival Style influenced details on this late 1920s residence. The rounded forms, including an undulating parapet and arched openings are accentuated by a pressed metal roof over the window bay.

SFHD #1 Lot 31
Built circa 1930–1942.

This 1930s Territorial Revival adobe home blends Mediterranean Style details including a deeply recessed arched door opening with an adjacent arched nicho window and black wrought iron elements. The hand-carved St. Francis of Assisi, patron saint of Santa Fe, was completed by resident owner Gaspar M. Naranjo in 2002.

SFHD #1 Lot 58
Front portion built pre-1885.
Back portion built circa 1921–1930.

The original Spanish-Pueblo Style is represented here with an adobe structure placed at the sidewalk edge. The unadorned hand-finished surfaces display an organic quality that plays with light and shadow.

Acknowledgements

First of all, we appreciate one another for being open enough to collaborate and sticking out the effort involved in this compelling project. Secondly, we thank David A. Rasch. Without additional clues and on first sight, David recognized with delight the historic buildings from our images, and educated us with his documentation of the architecture. We are grateful to Stuart A. Ashman for accepting our invitation to write the Introduction. We felt his perspective on the artwork and neighborhood from the point-of-view of Santa Fe's culture would add to the book. To Pat French, Lisa Samuel, and Robert and Ling Hilgendorf—your positive comments about every aspect of the book have added to our satisfaction in completing it. Thanks, too, to Elaine Bergman, Executive Director of the Historic Santa Fe Foundation, for her enthusiasm and encouragement when visiting us on Staab Street to see our house and our images in the early stages of developing the collection. She also kindly took time recently to talk about and give feedback on our mockup of the book. Other people whom we thank for what you know you generously did are Frank Nudo and Joseph Franklin. Thanks to Jim Smith and Carl Condit of Sunstone Press for seeing what we hoped they would in our initial presentation.

Victoria's personal thanks begin with family. To my father, Leon E. Rogers, for his example to strive always for one's best, to "carpe diem," and especially for the joy he expresses in sharing my accomplishments. To my sister whose keen sensibilities in life and the arts have had a lasting, valuable influence. To my grandmother who gave me a special feeling for old houses by making hers warm and inviting with her cooking and love. Thanks to my very dear, supportive friends, who are as busy as I am but always come through. And most of all, thanks to Cal for letting my all-consuming ideas and visions become his call to action, bringing his special genius to creating with me and producing our next reality.

Cal thanks my daughter Sunny for information on the latest technology for publishing when it was needed. Thanks to my father whose unwavering work ethic was instilled in me at an early age and for his knowledge of construction that helped shape my interests and was used in understanding the architecture in this book. And finally thanks to Victoria for her unrelenting support for everything I want to be.

Neighborhood street signs.

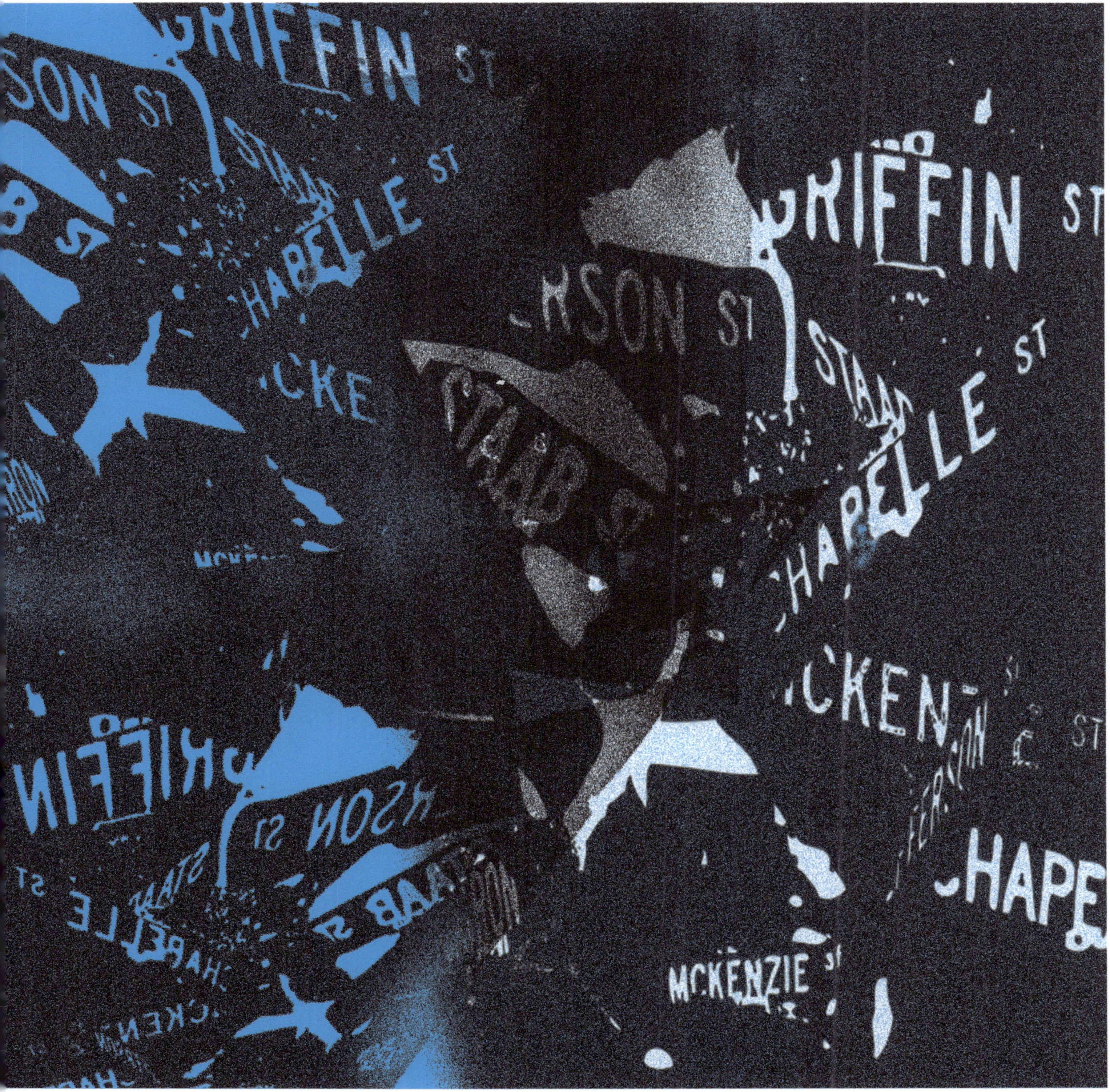
GRIFFIN ST
STAAB ST
CHAPELLE ST
MCKENZIE

About the Artists

Creative collaborators Victoria Rogers and Cal Haines were enticed gradually but steadily into the work that has resulted in this book. Victoria's originality and eye for color, composition and refinement combined adeptly with Cal's technical, improvisational and rhythmic design skills gave the artists a dynamic toolbox. The first "vision" (of the McKenzie House) turned into many inspired walks and more images of the neighborhood architecture, leading to an adventure of meeting historic guardians and preservationists, hunting through City of Santa Fe files, researching and writing. The entire process took on a challenging and rewarding life of its own.

Prior to this time, Victoria Rogers has been best known as an artist for her portfolio of color landscape photography with selections archived in the New Mexico Museum of Fine Art's historic Jane Reese Williams Collection. Rogers's multifaceted mind is apparent in her professional story. She started out as a realtor, earned a double master's degree in Teaching the Visually Impaired, was editor on several arts publications, is a retired Registered Nurse, active massage therapist, property manager and concert event presenter. She spent a good many years dreaming up a future that is now happening.

Cal Haines is a lifelong jazz drummer whose multidimensional thinking patterns find additional expression through photographic and abstract representations of auditory experiences. Before the McKenzie project, his pictures were primarily of performing musicians, conveying the feeling of playing and listening to music. Cal's appreciation for architectural forms got an early start on the apprentice track with his grandfather and father, both master masons. He chose a career in semi-conductor engineering, continuing to perform music and to develop artistically. Cal is a high-energy, high-stimulation individual, and now that he has officially retired, he is able to work more intensively on his passion for the drums and explore other mediums as well.

In a short time as collaborators, longtime Santa Fe resident Victoria Rogers and Cal Haines have been featured in *Albuquerque The Magazine*, as Featured Artisans on an interior design website, and in a documentary film about artists and the muse. Their websites are: victoria-rogers.com, calhaines.com and.newcanstudios.com.

Victoria Rogers

Cal Haines

The body typeface is Adobe Caslon Pro, first released by William Caslon in 1722 and based on seventeenth-century Dutch old style designs. The first printings of the American Declaration of Independence and the Constitution were set in Caslon.

Display type is Trajan, an old style typeface re-interpretated in 1989 by Carol Twombly. Based on the letterforms used for the inscription at the base of Trajan's Column from which the typeface takes its name.

Printed on acid free paper.